DIN

DINOSAUR,

WHAT DO YOU SEE?

Thank you for buying this book!

Please consider leaving us a review.

We are a small business, but your review makes

a BIG difference!

Thanks in advance for your support!

Let's Begin!

Prehistoric trees,
Prehistoric trees,
what do you see?

We see a T-Rex,
as big as can be!

T-Rex, T-Rex, what do you see?

I see a Stegosaurus,
proud and free!

Stegosaurus,
Stegosaurus,
what do you see?

I see a Pterodactyl,
flying with glee!

Pterodactyl,
Pterodactyl,
what do you see?

I see a Triceratops,
strong and sturdy!

Triceratops,
Triceratops,
what do you see?

I see a Diplodocus,
munching veggies!

Diplodocus,
Diplodocus,
what do you see?

I see a Plesiosaur, swimming freely!

Plesiosaur,
Plesiosaur,
what do you see?

I see a Woolly Mammoth,
stomping loudly!

Woolly Mammoth,
Woolly Mammoth,
what do you see?

I see an Ankylosaurus,
armoured and spiky!

Ankylosaurus,
Ankylosaurus,
what do you see?

I see a Brachiosaurus,
tall and lanky!

Brachiosaurus,
Brachiosaurus,
what do you see?

I see a Spinosaurus,
long and spiny!

Spinosaurus,
Spinosaurus,
what do you see?

I see a Velociraptor,
quick and speedy!

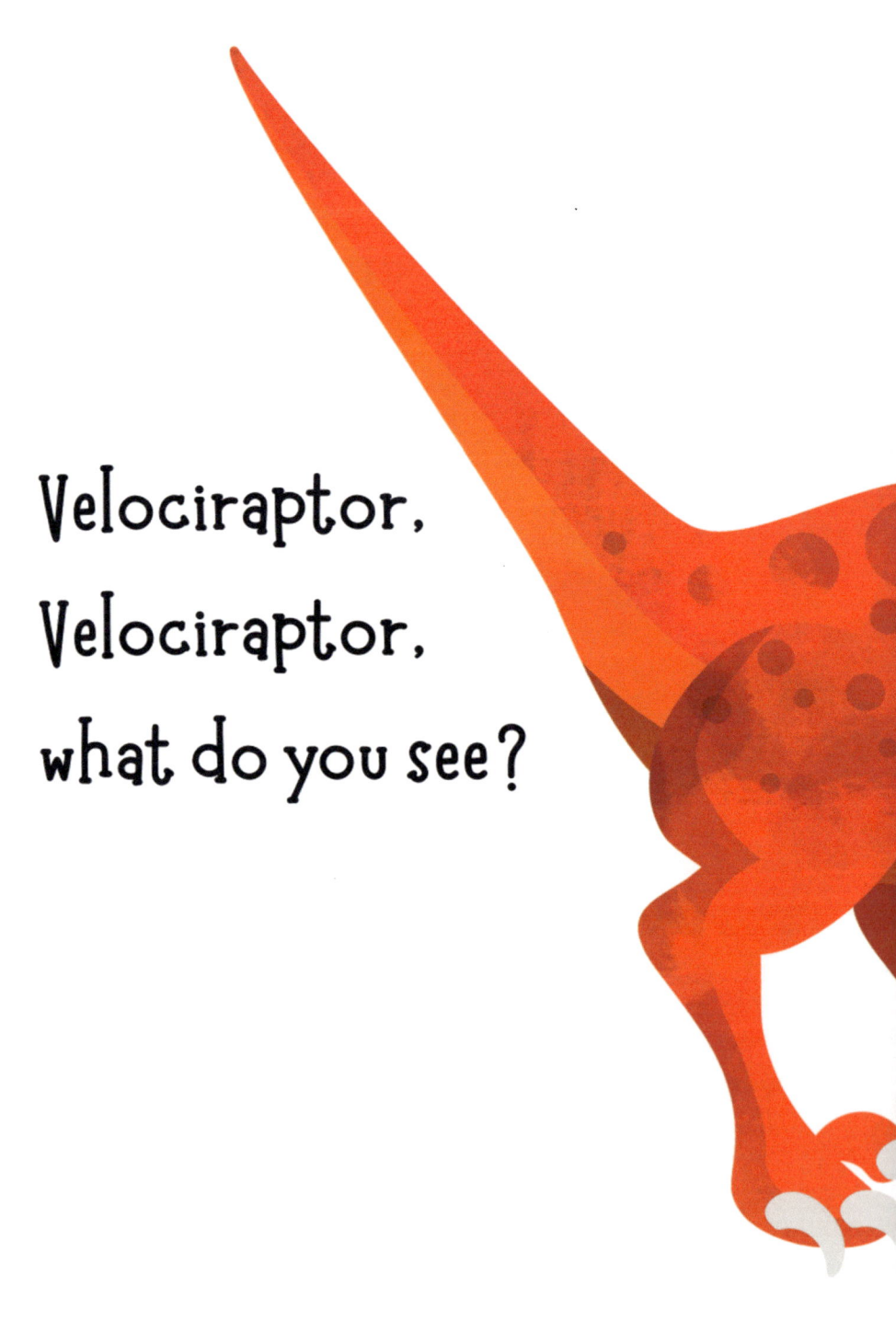

Velociraptor,
Velociraptor,
what do you see?

I see a Dinosaur egg,
just waiting to be!

Dinosaur egg,
Dinosaur egg,
what do you see?

I see a world
living in harmony!

Thank you!